AWAKENING THE GENIUS IN YOU

BY

REY ANTHONY

COPYRIGHTS 2021 REY RIVERA
ALL RIGHTS RESERVED.
NO PART OF THIS PUBLICATION MAY BE DISTRIBUTED OR COPIED IN ANY WAY PHYSICALLY OR/AND ELECTRONICALLY FOR FINANCIAL BENEFIT WITHOUT ASKING THE AUTHOR

INTRODUCTION

This book is created for people who feel they have nothing inside them that makes them believe in themselves. We all have a genius for our own benefit, it can be a simple one or a complex one. We all have one genius on us. What matters in this life is to find where to develop it and understand it in order to promote all possible measures and reach that maximum level of genius. I don't think I'm a genius in all my skills but I search every day how to find my genius constantly. With discipline I have been able to overcome the best battles of my life. The same battles can be had by you and the same genius can be had by you, based on your identity. I want you to achieve what you want in life, no goal is simple, they are all important. You are important. Thanks to the exercises that I am going to explain in this book, I have been able to cope with loneliness, poverty, mental health issues, and physical health issues. Some basic and some high level. If it weren't for this discipline I wouldn't have made it.

The world is advancing, evolving and socializing faster. We are living in a more exposed social life. It is of the utmost importance and of utmost necessity to connect with oneself and to know oneself. Society shouldn't choose who we are, we should choose who we want to be based on our happiness. With so many daily distractions we forget who we really are and who we can be, that's going to get better today. Write down today's date.

By doing this book I am out of my comfort zone. Many times I thought about it, many times I started it. Many times I doubted myself. Many times I was scared because of the vulnerable content it contains. So it took me two years to start this book. This book is my example of looking for the genius in me to share what I know. As I go deep into the writing of this book it lets me know what I have become to date. Because the person that I wanted to start with, I am not the same today. I mean with more necessary experiences that they had to go through.

Around the last 10 years I have met people from different cultures, thoughts, ideas, different ways of seeing life. Knowing who I really am and meeting so many people around the world I have been able to evaluate who I want to be or what defines me when handling different situations. Not in comparative terms. I have never liked the comparison of comparing myself with other people. Example: "if I want to be better than other people" or "worse than other people". My quest is to impact my own life while I live.

My memory at this precise moment of so many people with whom I have shared my thoughts. They advised me to write books with my life experiences and with my ideals. If you are one of those people who recommended it to me, I finally did it. I do so with much honor to your advice. Your advice was spinning in my mind all these years. You believing in me, made me believe in myself even more. I never thought to do it at this time, if they had asked me before. Life has prepared me for everything I am going to say here. Errors and solutions. Ups and downs. Life put me to the test to be able to carry the message. To learn the same that I applied today.

Many people think, including you, that to be a genius or to be happy, life has to be "perfect". But "perfect" can have so many simple meanings that you haven't noticed. Your life begins to be "perfect" when you accept the imperfection of life. Yes, it sounds crazy but it's the truth. Many people put their BIG goals on hold to wait to "get it right." Basically, "being well" is achieved by not putting goals on hold. Whoever wants a "perfect" progress better not even try to progress because it is not. The great geniuses of world history, those who have impacted the world so that you and I have the accessible life that we have today, have made mistakes thousands of times to achieve the goal. With this said, being a genius does not mean being perfect. It doesn't mean having a perfect life, it means perseverance and acceptance.

- INTRODUCTION
- EXPIRED CULTURE
- HOW TO PICK THE NEW PEOPLE AROUND YOU.
- FINANCIAL DISTRIBUTION
- POSSIBLE MONEY SOURCES
- NFT
- "AFFILIATE MARKETING"
- "DROP SHIPPING"
- AIRBNB(renting a property you don't own)
- CONTENT CREATOR
- MENTORING
- DELEGATE
- TURO
- GARAGE SALES
- THE MODERN ERA
- WHY SPEAK ON SOCIAL MEDIA EVEN IF NOBODY KNOWS YOU?
- THE MENTAL AND EMOTIONAL HEALTH
- THAT YOU HAVE WITHIN YOUR DIGESTIVE SYSTEM
- THE MISSION
- I WANT TO MEET YOU

YOUR EXPIRED CULTURE

This is the most "controversial" topic I've been able to touch on in recent years. Culture is something that is respected and I respect it, but because of culture many people do not fulfill their dreams and worse do not dare to dream. Culture creates beliefs in you that life is "one way" but if you go after dreams, you have to detach yourself from "your culture". That's why it sounds controversial when I mention it. It has nothing to do with losing your essence, who you are and what you believe in. It is that your habits are going to separate from your culture and your beliefs.

I'm going to explain a little better. When I talk about these types of issues I mean.

Examples:

When a baseball player has a son, he wants his son to be a baseball player. When a Doctor has a son, he wants his son to be a Doctor. When a teacher has a son, he wants his son to be a teacher.

I speak of children but it can be family or friends, whoever.

The equation is repeated for generations making a "bubble" in knowledge of what life can really be when it comes to progress and when it comes to surviving. I go back and repeat to make clear, I don't want to say that a teacher, a Doctor or a baseball player isn't progressing, it is. Of course it is. What I mean is that a line of thought that does not change from generation to generation is ancient knowledge. Because they focus so much on the career or what is "normal" based on what they know. Do this exercise, ask parents of children or people who are expecting children, *what do you want your child to be?* Or basic: How *do you want the people around you to be?* List how many mention "happy" before anything. So you will realize how society is hurt. We are in an era in which each person must choose or can choose what truly makes them happy. But most people grow up not knowing that and there are those who die without knowing it. Like everything in life, there may be people who are great professionals in what they want to be, but at the last minute they don't feel happy with their profession or happiness in general. That comes at the root because they did what they were told to do and not what they loved to do.

Some people suffer with many benefits, but there are other people who suffer for doing what they are told and 0 benefits. Right now you have to think who are you? What happened to you? Who do you want to be? If you look at your life right now, are you where you want to be? Are you doing what you want to do or are you doing what they want you to do? That's how serious the decision is to detach yourself from your culture for a moment to improve your decisions. To what makes you happy to do, what you love. You won't regret it in the future. The older generations have passed on the ancient knowledge for 100 years or more, the education that continues today. It is not the education you need to survive in life. Many say "education begins at home" so I wonder why us has to go to school. The education that you learned in school did not teach you to survive in life, to solve problems, to be happy, to create and materialize your dreams, to respect other people, to be empathetic. And the list would be infinite if I continue. The generations before come from an abuse of power creating fear. Mental and social corruption is basically what is deposited in your mind. And that is what you share. But that will change today. Imagine spending years in education and not knowing how to be happy or empathetic with others. Those are lost years, so is being a diplomat just a topic? If you want to work on your own terms, traditional school education falls far short. As I said before, education within the home is also corrupted. They have the same education as you and that is why making wrong decisions is passed from generation to generation. Those of us who work to find our genius are ready and available to change our future.

Changing the future of the generation that is on the way is our mission every day. Making a book like this or raising your voice using social media is to wake up people. Everything is possible by changing what your culture has taught you these previous years.

It's never too late. Do not look for the fault of something or someone else's fault. I can't blame it now on what you weren't taught and you can't blame anyone. It's your fault if you don't want to learn new methods to improve your life. It's your fault if you learn new methods to know how to improve your mindset. I can speak for myself and my colleagues in the entrepreneurship industry. Many different backgrounds, good families or bad families, the education is the same, old. In my personal case, I learned to be a barber because of my mother and her interest in styling. When I decided to go to university to study a university degree, I decided on Criminal Justice, that was my father's interest. I failed at both. For the fact of picking and selecting something that I truly did not want. Since I needed to survive, I was a barber, 10 years to be exact. I don't regret the time I was a barber because it was the economic bridge to start each of my dreams of life that I have. I always knew it was temporary. It's crude that I had to say things like that. That I wasn't happy and I know it now because when I had the concept of happiness it was wrong. Because it was based on what I knew at the moment. But the quicker I accept what doesn't make me happy, the quicker I can choose what makes me happy. I accept that most of my failures or unhelpful thoughts were the fault of the old education, not the fault of the people who delivered the message. I lived most of my childhood and adolescence without knowing what a teenager needed or what was needed for a future adulthood.

It took me by surprise to take charge of my life from a very young age and I accepted it because I had no other choice. I could do two things, I could be the victim of my past or I could be superior to myself. I chose to be superior. I chose to improve my life at all costs. As I grew up, my environment was totally different from what it is now. In my childhood and adolescence I believed that decision-making was made with being aggressive and shouting to people who got in my way. I had too many miserable moments arguing with people. But when you don't know it, you think that this is "normal". Arguing is normal. Being in a bad mood is "normal." Disrespecting someone is "normal". There really is no exact line to define normal but that was not good, I'm sure. I also grew up thinking that my life was difficult and without a solution, but yes, I never accepted that it was my "normal". That is why I inform you that if your life is difficult right now at this precise moment it is because of your old education and because of your culture but it is not your fault, it is not your "normal". It can be much better I assure you. I'm being reserved on super general and basic topics. There are no ways to measure what is "normal" by comparing cultures, because in other places it is normal to eat toads from the lake.

You can begin to normalize believing in yourself,with that you can be happy and free. In other cultures they have no choice but to be loyal to the culture out of obligation and maybe they don't know what they can improve on. Because they do not accept that there is something better outside of that culture. Thanks to acceptance you enjoy cultures and differences. You can see the difference in how difficult it is for other people to live and between what is "difficult" for one person and what is "normal" for another.

Every time you have the opportunity to speak with different cultures in different languages from different parts of the world, we understand that knowledge is something infinite, just like happiness. These are two things that many people believe and grow up thinking that this is limited, that life has to be one way, happiness has to be in something specific and there is nothing external. It's wrong.

There are great people, with great thoughts, with great hearts who can help the world in a better empathetic way, in a better entrepreneurial way, and they haven't been able to do it. They have not been able to know their inner genius because of their belief and because of their cultural loyalty. That's what makes me sad. Never let your essence be corrupted by something that has nothing to do with you. You have your own way. For many people, leaving their culture and their traditional thought to their people believe that it is betrayal. But you cannot betray yourself by taking care of something that limits you from knowing your great potential.

I have loved every step of my growth and more to make peaceful decisions for the good of myself without having to argue and without having confrontations with people. It has been one of the great blessings of my change.

It was not easy at all to grow in a bad mood and change to calm. It took me a lot of understanding to learn empathy and I am still learning to value empathy. It took me years to get to know that peaceful version of myself and I don't regret it because it separates me from so many problems with other people. People who live arguing by nature that it is not worth spending energy on that. Now I used my courage in productive things like getting better and being more disciplined. Yes I accept it, giving up my culture and giving up my beliefs has made me a better human being. It has brought me closer to being the person I always dreamed of.

Lack of knowledge affects love and finances. There are too many people who justify that this is "normal" and do nothing about it. Together they use the excuse "This life they left us, we cannot make another way of life".

It takes too much courage to change those terms. Stop being an aggressive person and stop being a poor person, that is the mission. Many people live in fear, fear also that was created by the Government or Leaders from the past who use leadership. They want people afraid of the economy and very afraid of progress because they simply want to take advantage of the fact that people remain silent in fear so that they can do their damage. From generation to generation from the highest point in society from the lowest point in history. It is convenient for the government that you do not have knowledge so that you believe that all your rights are legal and violating your rights at the same time. I really don't know what is sadder, living a corrupt life that cuts your wings so you can't grow or knowing that your wings are being cut and you don't want to do anything to grow. I am going to leave this line of thought to your discretion, these new decisions that you are going to make in your life to improve.

Start by evaluating your life for yourself, not for those around you. Not because of what they tell you to do. If you are where you want to be OK but if there is something that worries you, you deserve the change you are looking for. The change you are looking for in this book has always been within you, I am only the bridge to remind you of it. I realized that I was in a bad culture, talking to myself in times of loneliness, I questioned myself that life could not be like this, so I looked for an answer. Life gave me the opportunity to be a barber with many clients, with many lines of thought in order to better understand life, psychology and what was really happening to me. Not in terms of comparing myself because as I told you at the beginning I don't like to compare myself with anyone. But to know what I want to be happy, I needed to know what happiness was first in the terms that I wanted or wanted to start. I feel good when I start to meet people with better empathy for me. When I began to meet people with the same entrepreneurial vision as me, then I understood that there is more life ahead. Believe me if you have a question, a doubt about how your life can be better, <u>the answer exists</u>. We are already living in such a modern world today that now it is easier than it was for me. I had to drink my own way with my own mistakes and also mistakes of other people that affected my growth. When you keep meeting people you understand who wants to see you well or who wants to do you good, as well as who wants to see you bad and who wants to do you bad at the same time. These are things that you must evaluate closely because someone always wants to get involved in progress to prevent you from progressing due to bad culture. If you don't know empathy, you're going to struggle with every person who gets in your way. That is why your mission is also to know peace. Peace of mind and empathy will help you fight for your goals and not with the people who get into your battle. People who want to fight just want to fight, they don't want to progress, it's not the same. It's not worth it, it's not worth the cost of your energy or the cost of your peace. When you are separating from your culture the hardest part is separating perhaps from your loved ones. Where your influence, your love and most likely what you know about life has grown.

When you open your eyes you begin to question what is happening or how you can improve and there comes the mental debate that "*things are not like that, there is no possible change*". At that moment, if you start debating with the opinions of people who do not have the same vision as you, you are losing the battle yourself. Obviously, since you are a person with a good heart, you want to improve. You want the people around you to improve too, but if they don't want to learn the new economy or new knowledge, they won't adapt to what you say. They will see you as "*crazy*" or as "*impulsive*", as "*ambitious*" or whatever name they give you so you don't even try something different to them. That is the first battle in awakening your new you. My advice is that you communicate what you feel but do not fight with anyone, continue with your legacy, continue looking for your happiness, continue looking for the genius in you. That requires all your possible energy to be able to accept your new culture, accept your old culture and it will help you a lot to relieve the mind of bad thoughts. To progress you have to have a clear mind free from emotional problems and free from arguments with another type of human being who is not the same as you. The quicker you accept that the quicker you can be happy in making decisions to move forward. It's not going to be easy any day, that's why I say, whoever wants to progress without having ups and downs shouldn't do it. There are too many people who are tied to the culture who are tied to people and are not tied to their progress and die inside wanting to progress. Wanting to touch those goals, wanting to make that trip, wanting to say I love you to that person who has always wanted to say I love you but they don't. When you understand the line between respect for yourself and the fact that other people's differences towards you do not affect you, it is at the moment that you are ready to walk steadily. That will start today. You're going to be afraid that they won't accept you with your new line of thinking. Sure, I'm not saying no, but fear is normal in any kind of change. That fear is temporary while the benefit is lasting when you decide to be you. It is worth the decision but remember to respect the line of thought of others so that people respect yours. Go find that genius in you, it's about time. If we keep talking about this topic we will never finish because it is an unlimited chain of situations that affect the peace and mental health of millions of people. When it comes to victims of mental and physical abuse it is the worst. These abusers believe that emotional abuse or physical abuse is "normal" and it is not. **If you are experiencing emotional or physical abuse, ask for help right now,** be it a man or a woman, because there are different types of abuse in different ways that do not help you to be happy, that do not help you to be calm, that corrupt your peace. That is part of an ancient culture just like racism, like many bad things for the human being that have corrupted millions of boys, girls, women and men. That is something <u>that will change if you ask for help in time</u>. Do not be afraid to leave where you are, do not be afraid to move forward for progress without abuse.

There are many people waiting to love you, there are many people waiting to support you. You don't have to waste any more time on emotional abuse based on an ancient culture. Because you love your culture, because you love your background doesn't mean you have to do something that doesn't make you happy and live in a toxic environment. Why live in a toxic environment for love of country or for love of fear? It will turn your most toxic days and the results are: insecurity, guilt and all those things that exist within the emotions to lose control of your direction to be a genius. I repeat, it doesn't have to be like that, you can go the extra mile, you can ask for help, you can search within yourself for what makes you happy and who your true identity is, and from there start a new path together. Think about it when you are lonely thinking about what you are going to do with your life, asking yourself if it is worth changing your life, if it is worth the risk of changing. Asking for help in life is the direction you are looking for, you already found it but without action you are not going anywhere. So fill yourself with power, write down your goals and find the way. There are so many things that have been damaged in the world because of stereotypes. For me, the real magic that exists is to live outside the stereotypes. That does not mean betraying your culture or betraying your essence. Living outside the stereotypes will give you the opportunity to live a life in which to make yourself happy regardless of what others think. However, living within the stereotypes is living only thinking about pleasing others. It will make you unhappy. There are many ways to explain these situations and you will have yours in particular. The psychological or psychiatric disorder that comes with the passage of time is also repeated from generation to generation and will continue to exist. You don't have to be a Doctor or a researcher to realize it. But I repeat we are here to live the best way based on the times we are living now and we cannot live in the past we have to live in the present. Accumulating points for the future, that future in which you are going to shine, that future that is waiting for you with a lot of love, with a lot of desire and with a lot of success.

HOW TO PICK THE NEW PEOPLE AROUND YOU.

Based on the topic we were talking about recently. Once you make the change you want to change in your culture, you want to change the people around you and you want to take a new direction. Looking for people and different things you have to be super selective with who you are going to have in your circle. When it comes to surrounding yourself with new people, you have to understand that you have to protect your new inner energy and your new inner peace. That helps not to make the same mistake of the past repeatedly. I have seen different people around the world make the same mistake of putting certain people's characteristics on a pedestal. That's what I mean by how they look on the outside. For example, there are people who want people around them who have money or look like they have money. There are people who want to surround themselves only with people who have tattoos. There are people who want to hang out with people who dress in the latest fashions and the list goes on and on. That they have the same body or hair color in the same way. For tastes, the colors of course yes. Desire who you want to relate to but don't forget things much more important than the external image, if you forget it it will cost you time and peace.

Outward beauty or desired characteristics can be misleading in many ways. You may have something visually pleasing like enjoying the natural landscapes of the earth but not the results of what you really seek or need in your current life to progress on external body characteristics. Human beings and all living beings are perfect on this earth regardless of disabilities but obviously we create images or desires of who one wants to relate to based on visual pleasure or what is believed to be visual pleasure in any way if you are a man or woman. Many people think or imagine that when they need to progress they need to be happy first and they think that to be happy they need to have people around them or a specific person. Looking for people to have around you is time and energy that you dedicate. You can't spend more time looking people you want around you than you spend time with yourself first before exposing yourself to more people. You cannot confuse loneliness with a lack of company in the sense that if you are alone or alone with somebody you will feel better or will do better. So this is when you put images or visual pleasures aesthetically before progress, before empathy or the love you feel for yourself and for others. That's where you make the mistake of choosing the wrong people. That mistake that can consume you years that you were trying to overcome. Years perhaps of understanding that it was one more mistake that you wanted a change from.

Imagine *someone* who wants to have a person by his side and in all the characteristics that he wants to be all aesthetically exterior without any quality inside. It would be filling your visual pleasure but visual pleasure is not what is needed to build dreams, the brain is needed more than anything else. Seeing the process and the proces most of the time is ugly in the road of success. That same "*someone*" chooses another person with exterior qualities and ignoring the interior ones, he/she will not know what ancient culture that person comes from. When it comes to meeting people, putting the exterior of people first on the scale will not know the damage that may come along the way when that person really opens up completely and lets you know what beliefs he/she has and how he/she sees life. Today there are very few people who open up from the beginning if they are good people because they want to take care of themselves and yet there are those who don't even care to open up.

Let's talk about examples: on the issue of racism they don't say it first, they say it over time with their attitudes or comments. An abusive person is not going to tell you that they are abusive from day one. Those red flags are not seen from the beginning if you do not understand the personalities of the human being or cultures, much less if you value only the exterior. Each person has significant value, but don't let your own visual desires kill your value. I want you to understand with this point that you want people in your life, in your progress, beyond the aesthetic and when you describe your circle it begins with characteristics such as love, people who love themselves and love humanity. Have ambition in empathy.

People who give you support, who give you understanding. People who really want to help you without anything in return. Characteristics that are worth much more than any exterior image. Use the example of a blind person: the imagination of how beautiful or not can be based on what the blind person believes. The blind person naturally begins to value more internal things such as touch feeling, how they speak to them, how they treat them and how they help them. Because all of those things help you progress based on that type of disability. It is the best descriptive example of what I mean. One must choose people as if blind and not blindly having eyes. If you are blessed to have eyes, don't waste them. If you use your blessing having eyes and the ability to choose the people you want to interact only for visual pleasure, you are not playing for your team. You are not playing for yourself. There are so many people fighting over time because they "can't find" their ideal person based on a visual image, that's sad. If you choose a person and they help you and if you don't help them back, that person disappears, it's not for you. You deserve a person who is in the good and the bad. That has empathy for what you went through or what you go through as well as you have equal empathy with that person and with people. I mean we should meet people with a lot of respect for who they are. Value them as they are with the imperfections they may have based on the ancient culture and their beliefs, but be able to reach terms that help them progress together regardless of whether it is visually pleasing or not. The visually pleasing will not take you from where you want to go today. Maybe some people can give you second hand pleasure of what you are looking on the outside but not what you are really looking for inside that is first. If you are looking for something that lasts and loyalty in people around you, you cannot prioritize the exterior of a person. Choose people around you who love you and value you no matter what.

I understand this issue not only by talking to so many people, I have experienced prejudice firsthand. Many times I was ignored for being a lonely person. I was ignored for not coming from a family of money or a family that was not united. Today I understand how empty those people have lived to judge me for those simple things without truly knowing me and not giving me the opportunity. I also remember when I arrived at places with my first car that was not aesthetically luxurious, it was quite the opposite and I saw people in the distance laughing at me. Looking at me as if I were less because of the car I was driving. People did not believe in me because of my profession as a barber. Of course I have lived by many prejudices.

The path to progress for me has been difficult from the beginning because of those things that people observed about me on the outside and did not give me the opportunity to value my insides. Today I thank each person who has taught me how it feels to be ignored or judged because in the same way I learned how it feels to be loved and valued and to know the difference. There is a big difference in those two terms. That's why whoever wants to see you well, whoever wants to help you, won't care how you look or who you are. They are simply going to help each other from a good heart to another good heart. In the past I fell into that dark place of looking for visible pleasures that I didn't have, assuming that it was what I needed to be happy of fullfill and I was wrong. I put it in my head when I was alone in my childhood that my happiness depended on not being alone, but it never occurred to me that by looking for that I would get together with people who minus me and did not add value to me. What I was thinking in my adolescence? I didn't know what it was to be accompanied by people of value, I didn't know what value was anyway, I didn't know how to be alone with myself either. Based on mistakes, we understand that it is more pleasant to walk alone than to walk with people who do not add up. It is not difficult for me to accept it today. I proudly say that this stage passes. Perhaps you who are reading this also go through or have gone through the same thing or will go through the same thing in the future. Not everyone will understand the term entrepreneurship, that is why many people do not support entrepreneurship, but that is their fears, not yours. When you are growing your genius, making changes nobody close wants to see you win, nobody wants to be there living your process in their own blood, but at the same time when they see you growing they want to congratulate you. They even say that they know you personally but they do not help either way. In the end they want to do what you are doing or ask how you did it. When you needed them they were not there or they undervalued you. In the future they arrive without calling them. Life things.

Believe me, if you choose the wrong people to be by your side when it comes to progress and bring out the genius in you, they will want to bring you down with negativity and if you are a person who is not easy to lift emotionally, it will cost you twice as much. Not impossible but one more life lesson of acceptance. I'm telling you in all honesty, you don't know how many people have laughed at me and my goals. It can still happen from time to time. Goals I have achieved today that were just ideas on paper before. They have laughed at me to my face and told me to my face that I will never achieve anything in life. People have wished me a lonely life and even death itself. Many times that type of words or thought comes from the people you trust the most when you are starting your changes, opening your eyes. Over time, people find out who I am and without knowing me they can tell me the same or worse things on social media. What does this tell me? That these people talk about themselves do not talk about me, what they can say describes what is in their hearts, not mine. It has nothing to do with my reality or my future. This is life when you want to change, negative people find out that you are going to change and if you change. They will congratulate you on hypocrisy and others will hate you and a small percentage will be happy for you and will fight and cry your battles. Those who cry the battles with you never forget them. Write their names and do not leave them unattended. Those people are the most real that exist and they are very difficult to get back once you lose them. When I have the opportunity to talk to a person who helped me I constantly say thank you. It's something I can't help it. Those little helps can be a bridge and I know who they are always.

Better said, to those who do not want to grow, do not let them harm your evolution either. If there are people who do not value you and now you know it, do not say that life does not speak to you. Unfortunately, sometimes we fail in wanting to change people who do not want evolution because it means a lot the support of them. Because that is the unconditional support that you want from specific people, but sadly it doesn't work that way. Believe me you don't want to change people your way it doesn't work like that. With this I want to tell you that if a person does not support you and you want to fight for them to support you yes or yes or if you have an idea and people do not understand and you insist them to understand, it is a lost battle. Because if they don't have the vision or the belief that things are possible, that you can make a difference, they won't see in you that you can do anything. If people want to believe that you are nobody in life, let them believe it. When people don't believe in you, use that as an engine to push yourself and value yourself, not to show that you can for those specific people. The benefits are for you, not for anyone else. However, those same people who do not support you, in the future they will say "wow" he did it.

When you were down you were not valued by them, it will be very difficult for them to value you being up either. As I told you a while ago, you want people in your life who love you with your best battles and your worst battles too. Those are the people who truly love you.

I remember many people telling me that I wasn't going to achieve anything because I didn't have a college degree. Right now I'm wondering what I couldn't achieve without a college degree. Today hundreds of people come to me, many with diplomas and even PHDs to ask me advice on life. I do not mean by this that I have more knowledge or skills than a diplomatic person with a PHD's. We all need each other in some way to progress. People know something I don't know just like I know something they don't know. You should never judge someone for what they don't have or for what they have, you shouldn't judge anyone. We must as a mission value each person that exists in the world in an empathetic and respectful way. Imagine yourself humiliating a person because of how they look on the outside or because of the plans they have. That person is not yet fulfilled at the moment and years later that person is the one who may help you in the most difficult moments, YES that same person that you didn't believe or judge, OUCH!

That is why in this social life we have a lot of collective work to do as entrepreneurs and as individual geniuses in order to promote each person who is looking for their inner genius.

There is so much emotional abuse by disrespectful people of little mental quality towards people who want to make a difference. It is not that they are bumps on the road because they are not, but simply a distraction, not everyone is willing to go through that kind of distraction. There are people who are working on their strengths and weaknesses. There are weak people who stay on the weak side because those people around want to constantly put their finger in wounds just to feel power, to feel the pleasure of humiliation. That's why I tell you to learn to choose well, learn to choose who you want to grow, not debate. Fight for your groth and believe me, you do not need an external beauty from somebody to do that. You need courage and everything that your interior is capable of doing to achieve success. Every time you have an idea you want to share with your loved ones, it is understandable but at the same time understand that if they do not see the same vision of the idea. Please do not feel bad or guilty because of them thinking that your idea is bad (for them). If that is what you believe, you have to execute the idea, whether they believe in you or not. Do not let an opinion of a person without belief in entrepreneurship put weight on your genius awakening.

Imagine if I told a person that I want to make a book, perhaps this same book that you are reading now and told me not to do it because I am not a well-known person. Also tell me that no one is going to read it and I should not spend my time and energy. I really have to listen to that person? I trust that by making this book I can reach anyone, even one. I believe in myself no matter how many people tell me not to do it because I already did it. And maybe my goal is not for millions of people to read it, maybe my goal is to finish something for myself.

Let's talk a little history. The culture of your background 50, 60 years ago, maybe 100 years ago, men spent their entire childhood listening *"when you grow up you go to war or to the army"*. In their adolescence their only option was to have to go to war. There were almost no other plans if it was a man. If she was a woman, her only option to live had to be a nurse or a housewife. Also both victims of slavery around the world.

Other times peoples option was survive massacres of the holocaust by hiding inside the walls, leaving the country without knowing when gonna see their family again. And at the same time on the other side of the story you wake up to kill these people without mercy. Imagine how much trauma these people grow up with and pass it down from generation to generation, it's horrible. Thinking about it, I know that there are many people who today do not survive those horrible times.

Today there are people who have a horrible day if they do not receive "likes" on their social media. This time is creating another type of unnecessary trauma for not raising wisdom. In the old days *YOU HAD NO CHOICE* and now you can decide what affects you and what doesn't.

We must be grateful for the times we are living. Today you have everything accessible and you are one button away from changing your life. A button you can order food. A button you can instantly transfer money worldwide. Maybe you are one button away from meeting the love of your life, who knows. The list goes on. We are in the best time to live. If you really want to understand and bless your life, analyze your life with the culture of before vs. now and stop complaining.

The older generation grew up with the idea that they could only make one decision in their lives. That was the way and no more. That's why all the decisions that people who want to make a difference and work on their own terms, share what they think with one of these old mind people and quickly think that it would be crazy to be different. People like this are already used to doing only one thing and that's not bad, that's what they believe. What is not fair is when those people who do not believe in themselves because of what they believe and want to get in the way of the goals of other people who want to build a different future. When you are going to talk about your goal or your idea, you have to be very delicate with whom you share it so that you are not going to confuse a person who does not understand you for something that does not support you. Basically if doesn't understand you and lets you know what thinks but it has nothing to do with not supporting you or anything to do with your future.

Use the rule of five people, if you get together with five people you will be the sixth of those with whom you get together. If you get together with five people who are poor, you will be the sixth. If you get together with five entrepreneurs, you will be the sixth. Seek to share your ideas with people who add value to your idea. If you don't have anyone to share your idea with, share it with me, write to me on any of my platforms and I'll attend to you. If you feel alone in life I will attend to you. I know what it is to feel alone. I know what it is to feel that you have no hope in life. I know what it feels like that all your ideas are wrong or that your path in life is wrong or a promising future. It is desperate to ask for help in terms of direction. Whenever you speak to life and the universe that a person appears to give you faith, arrives. However, if you don't have anyone looking around you right now, you don't have anyone to share that idea with or how you feel, look at the blessing you have that you can share it with me. Look how awesome your life is because you are already connected with someone through a book. If you were given this book, it has a special meaning because that person who gave it to you wants to see you well. That is a person you want to keep close. Everything has a purpose in life, nothing happens outside of mathematics, outside of the equation. If you have an idea in mind because you want to achieve it and not just want to achieve it, you can achieve it. I'm telling you, I've gone from being alone without hope to having a community that not only makes me feel more complete, they value me, look after me, are looking out for me. I receive messages every day from different parts of the world thanks to that I was able to raise my voice of who I genuinely am and what I want in life with the right people. It is not difficult to know that there are more humans when you are alone, you are not alone. But I don't blame you, I thought the same as you. I thought I was going to be alone all my life because they told me that too many times. They told me that I was going to finish lonely just because I was a person who had goals and no one was going to understand my goals. That if I achieved them, I was going to end up with only my goals but unhappy. Those words were said to me, many times. If we are weak-minded we begin to believe it only because we are in a vulnerable moment.

You have to put a lot of effort, a lot of discipline when they tell you that you can't build anything. Accept that you are different and that not everyone is going to want you to succeed.

When you are vulnerable these words can hurt you but if you are aware and have your feet on the ground you realize that what these people are talking about is their reality and not your reality. It never has to do with your reality, a person who tells you that you can't do something never has to do with you.

Right now I remember someone years ago telling me that I was a "dreamer" based on my goals. When they tell you that, it's basically to your face that they tell you not to even try. At that time my goals have been my engine to move forward and maybe at that time it hurt me. I accept it. With the passage of time, awakening my conscience, I realized that person was right, I am a dreamer. Dreamer who achieve their goal. I get what I want. I achieved what I plan to do and analyzing it well now, it was not a criticism as I thought. It was a comment of admiration and thanks to that admiration is that I can exercise what I want. That comment turned out to be my fuel. If I accept it, I'm a dreamer. Once I accepted being a dreamer, I accepted that I want to work on my own terms at the time I want, at the pace I want everything is easier. Imagine yourself thinking that you have an idea and that you cannot achieve it, that does not combine. However, there is a force within you that was the same that created the idea and the goals you have today will create the force and the path to achieve it.

FINANCIAL DISTRIBUTION

Now that you have decided to understand the ancient culture, you already know where you are in your present. You already know where you want to continue the path, now it's time to be realistic with yourself. What are your goals? Find a notebook and write them down right now. Now, since you have them, some come at no economic cost and some come at an economic cost. Let's start with those that do not have an economic cost and that is what you want to improve about yourself in terms of how you think and see life. For Example, you want to be more loving, respect yourself more, be more honest, empathic, etc. Whatever helps you with your inner emotions first. That's key honestly. That will help you make better decisions in which they are economic goals. Let's talk about those that have an economic cost. Let's start having realistic goals. By economic goals I mean to make money with money, not to have goals to spend money. Well, if that's what you want to do go ahead. There are people who want to find meaning in their work to stay alive but not with freedom. There are too many people trying to have a financial goal to feel good about unnecessary expenses. Like excessive designer clothes, a late-model car, a mortgage that compromises your entire salary. There are people who spend 30 years of their lives thinking that's what they work for, to have those 3 things until they die. Your financial goals first have to start by organizing your current financial goals. If you haven't done this in your life, I urge you to do it now using a digital or handwritten chart. With the table you can see the numbers better. You don't have to be an expert. If you are not an organized person because basically you are writing down in your notebook but you are still a disorganized person, the table will help you to have everything organized by obligation. Write down how much you are earning. Many people live check by check and because they live check by check they think they have control of their finances because they know when they are going to earn. But when you don't write down how much you're fully earning, you really don't know exactly. Once you write down how much you are earning in the second column, you will put what you spend. All in one line down, mortgage, car, electricity, telephone, purchase and miscellaneous. In the third column the amounts. Now use the sum of how much you are earning and how much you have left over at the end of the month. Be sure to write down the things that you spend unnecessarily in the month like going out to parties, like buying a piece of clothing that you didn't need or maybe you needed for the party. Expenses like these cannot be forgotten because that is where unnecessary expenses come from and if you cannot bear that expense, you will use the credit card. That adds more payments to your monthly payment than you can actually earn. Spending more than you earn is not only compromising your money but even your time and the obligation of not being able to leave work. If you are going to use the credit card to pay for something because you do not have money, it will cost you more than the price due to interest. These few times that you do that can take you backwards. Once you have the table ready of your finances clear, then it's time to start planning. What expense are you going to sacrifice or what expense are you going to cut completely? It is not easy at first for anyone. Even more difficult for people who have a very high lifestyle, they have a hard time starting over because they have already built an ego. Calm down if it's you, the ego and finances have a solution. Once you start doing this things start to get better. So don't be afraid to start over because it's better to start structured than to try to start disorganized looking for something to come out. Start cutting out everything that is necessary, meals out for example. When you eat out you spend three times what that product is worth without cooking in the supermarket. Start cooking and eating from home, start going out less, consume less alcohol, buy less clothes, wear the same clothes every day. Believe me you will have a large part of your monthly money left over. This applies to any salary. I have known people earning a hundred thousand dollars a month and not being able to live because they compromised their entire salary. That extra money you gonna see when you organize, you always have it. That money now you are going to start using it for your new goals. Either to invest or to create more economy for yourself. It is not just saving because saving is not multiplied. You can create a different flow of money than the one that already leaves you money. You did not see this extra money because you were used to spending it in full and even more. Now if you want to quit your job or create more money you have to be organized. If you're not organized with what you have now, you're not going to be organized with more of it. Many people believe that working and earning money is spent automatically. They get paid and they love to stay at zero because they know that next week they are going to get paid. It is important as you look at the money extra and resist temptation. Remember that when you spend all the time without control you already have a habit of spending, now you need to have a habit of controlling expenses and growing the account. These adjustments not only strengthen your economy, they strengthen your mentality. Everything comes hand in hand and helps you to be stronger, because before you couldn't do it because you were weak. Now you are structured and you are creating discipline. Strengthening from everywhere to improve your life. On the new path many times you will be tempted to say "*I am going to spend a little of the money from the new savings.*" You will tell yourself in your mind "*I'll get it back*". If you fall into that temptation then it becomes a habit and repeats itself in the future. And you make that mistake again over the months. When you come to see everything that you could have evolved is now on pause/stop for not putting discipline. The real secret of growing a monetary amount is to accept that money does not exist. Think back to when you spent and didn't care. Now prepare it and don't mind either. Be strong because you are strong. Another secret is also knowing how to say *NO* to many things, to the things that you said Yes before. Start saying NO if you are invited to a place that brings expenses back into your life. If you are invited to hangouts that require expenses, remember to yourself that you have a long-term goal. All those inviting things are perhaps a short period of pleasure. Maybe by sacrificing so much time, like months, you get weak because you want to feel your "old life". That is the confusion of the meaning of life. You do not want a pleasure in your life that will last a short time, you want a pleasure that lasts for the rest of your life. A pleasure for life, yes. Remember you have suffered too much in your life to be repeating quick moments without long-term meaning in your life. You want a life that values you forever. The fact that you are sacrificing many things now to improve, does not mean that your life will be like this forever. This is temporary but if you do not know how to make those sacrifices your life will remain in what you want to improve forever in "another try". It depends on how much you earn, will depend on how long you are going to improve economically. How much it will improve your mental toughness. In that time you cannot compete with another person's time. A person who perhaps earns less than you or more than you. Remember that you are in your own economic process and in your own mental process.

How can you not be desperate if you are already desperate? If you are desperate, start feeling not desperate because the moment you are desperate you are going to make desperate decisions. Decisions that come with a lot of regret. Try to live each day remembering that your goal is long-term, it is a real change and it will not happen overnight.

You were born to be free not only with your body, mentally free to. You are already free with your body, don't be a slave to your mind. Your mental game you have to constantly raise it to make it bigger. In your life you eat to stay alive and healthy. Nourish the mind in the same way so that it continues to grow and continue to expand. Fill yourself with knowledge, fill yourself with belief in yourself so that you don't fail yourself again.

Since you are mentally strong and ready to make better decisions, there is a solution if you have problems with the time it may take to get to what you want. The solution is to find a second job temporarily and if necessary a third. It's funny when you tell a person to find a second job, they take it badly because they can't rest or they won't have time. However, those same people who botter this comment, you ask them about their habits and it turns out that there is time for parties and hangovers. There is time to watch TV after work and sleep late. So if they could sleep late in the same things that waste time but in something that generates more money, finances can improve. It's a matter of habit, it's a matter of discipline. Use your time to add more value. You can use the time to have more value in wisdom and more economic power. The benefits that you seek in these extra and temporary jobs are for you only. You are doing for yourself what perhaps no one would do for you, don't think about anything else. You are sacrificing yourself for the first time, before you sacrificed yourself all the time for others, using money to surprise others, using money to party with others. Now you are here for yourself, to invest in yourself, to have a better quality of life. When you want and start these extra jobs they will criticize you saying super negative comments but remember the first session of this book. They're talking about their fears, not yours. Don't worry about time either, time is different for everyone. If you think you are taking a long time and you are losing consciousness of time, think about your role models who may not do the same as you want but they inspire you. Lebron James, one of the best NBA athletes in history. For sure, the Hall of Fame. Took 9 years to win his first championship. Without a father to follow and one of the most hated people on the planet at the same time. Justin Bieber started out singing in the streets just like Ed Sheran. Both with platinum records today. The Kentucky Colonel of Kentucky Fried Chicken restaurants after his 60th birthday met success and meaning of his life with his secret recipe for fried chicken. Ray Kroc the founder of McDonald's came into his own after his 50th birthday after failing in multiple businesses and going bankrupt multiple times. Leonardo DiCaprio won his first Oscar after 12 years from 6 nominations. Are you going to complain because things don't work out for you in a month?

How great are you doing what you do every day? Greatness is there waiting for you don't want it to be overnight. Believe me if it's overnight you won't feel the sacrifice or the reward that greatness has waiting for you. Look at my example. I had started this book two years ago and I put a pause on it and it was worth it. In these two years I have grown more spiritually, economically and physically and it gave me all the experiences more than what I was looking for to start and finish this book. From the beginning everything had a purpose which made me stop but I didn't know it, now I know it. I did not continue the manuscript that I already had before. I started it again without having to see the old manuscript because I am a new person and a better version of myself than I was two years ago. With this I tell you that the goals are there, you are going to achieve it. What you have to do is go one step at a time. Now thanks to the fact that I took two more years you can benefit much better from my way when I expressing myself. When I started it I was struggling with learning to express myself the way I express myself today and it's all been one day at a time. Believe me, a person like me was not too many words, I was not a person to express my feelings correctly. My feelings lived for many years in disarray. Because of the fear of being judged for expressing my real feelings. I also didn't know if they were real because I honestly feel that many times I put my feelings on pause because I didn't see it as a priority. With this said, each one of us has their different struggles. I have already learned to express myself, to have patience, to meet my goals every day, to love what I do, to love my life and in the long run they are given little by little. The goals will never stop because having goals is the engine of my life, it is what keeps me that spark of feeling life when I get up. The same can happen with you, I am not better than you or superior to you. If you think you have no purpose in life, use goals as a purpose to get up every day. If you don't have goals you start to have a life that you don't love, you start to have a routine that you don't love and the burdens become heavier. If you have goals to structure your finances and your inner being, you begin to live what you love, no matter the sacrifice or the time it takes you are enjoying every step of your life. There is pleasure along the way even if it is overwhelming, it is worth every shot you give yourself.

POSSIBLE SOURCES OF MONEY

"I AM NOT A FINANCIAL ANALYST YOU ALWAYS NEED TO DIG DEEPER YOU NEED TO DO AND MAKE YOUR OWN DECISIONS."

In this topic I am going to give you several ideas in case the light bulb has not turned on for you, at least one topic will turn on. Each person works to his method between profit or loss. I mean that there are people who want to gain more time in their life and other people who want to earn more money or better still earn both. There is no simple way, it gets easier with experience. In some methods you need a lot of physical quality to be present on a schedule and punch. These are perhaps the ones that steal happiness from most people, physically and mentally. There are other methods that you do not have to be in a specific place, you can do it from anywhere in the world with the internet and most of the time requires more mental work. What do you want to do? What do you want to develop? I love the Stock Market, not just for the benefit, I like it and I know it is a subject not for everyone. Obviously the Stock Market has been around for a long time and has too much history and you don't need all the history to trade the markets, but if you want to know more directly about this topic, I recommend you get my other two books. *"Secrets of a Day Trader" and "Repeating Patterns"*. You can get both at www.patronesrepetidos.com. (spanish version only)

Obviously you want a pleasant change but if you want to solve what is happening now try to solve it forever and not temporarily. If you want to change your traditional physical job for a computer you have to be more patient than you normally are. You think that you don't have patience but you have created a brutal patience in these years that you have worked in a place where you don't want with a salary that you don't want. If you have patience and it is "TOP" what happens is that you deposit it in the place where you get used to it and where you are not used to it weighs you down. There is such a great source of money online that I am sometimes led to believe that there is so much physical business even without an online presence. If you do not have an "online" presence today it is difficult to grow an idea in the digital age. The phone is something that everyone has and you spend five hours a day on the phone as your lifestyle and maybe you don't even realize it. What if your very online lifestyle could make you money. Through your lifestyle and if you spend five hours on the phone or on the computer and you are not generating more money than you do now, it is simply because you do not want to learn. I'll give you a couple of ideas. Remember any basic or complicated idea in this term you need a lot of mental energy, concentration and getting used to that kind of work. It can be efficient but at the same time it can drown you mentally and financially. You have to find what you like, what you are passionate about and something that defines you as a person. It will be easier for you to choose where you want to deposit the energy in the new source of money. New to you and some not so new because they really aren't new, they've been on the market for more years and I don't know why many people find out now but that's life.

NFT

NFT corresponds to the acronym "non fungible token", which we can translate as "non fungible token" or "non fungible asset", or, what is the same, the meaning of NFT means that it is an asset that it is unique, it cannot be modified and it cannot be exchanged for another of equal value, because there would not be an equal one.

Digital art is starting to auction for hundreds of thousands of dollars. A trend that could make illustrations, videos and other digital works such as GIFs and memes worth millions of dollars and all thanks to a certification of authenticity and property called Non Fungible Tokens or NFT.

Think about it, the art of collecting has moved to digital. It's one of the craziest things happening right now. Because you can get many of these photos on Google and already, you have one but "It is not the original" directly from the artist. Yes, let me explain better, do you remember collecting sports cards, figures, wall paintings, shoes etc. Over time they increase in value, because that has basically moved to the digital world. Collectors are willing to pay hundreds of dollars for an image directly from the artist.

To date the largest marketplace to invest in these types of transactions publicly is www.opensea.io/. There are also private sales directly with the artists or creator. So if you are good at designing or even your own photography this is a market you can look at. And if you are a collector looking for the newest, this is a good theme.

"AFFILIATE MARKETING"

One of the easiest ideas that has been around for maybe more than 15 years. It requires time, energy, little or no capital. It consists of you joining a brand such as Best Buy, Amazon or hundreds of companies that have this opportunity. You promote a product in your Social Media, text message or by e-mail with a link prepared by them and you will receive a piece of commission for the sale of that product. Yes, it's that simple, you think you have to be "Influencers" to get money from the most recognized brands and it's not like that. If you go to the Best Buy or Amazon website for example, there is an area that says "Affiliate" and you make your account. They have video tutorials on how you can be an affiliate of them. Imagine you buy your favorite laptop. You are delighted with your laptop and with your affiliate link you share it saying that you love that product. Several people buy with your link and you receive a commission for those purchases. Amazon receives millions of visits per day, millions of clicks and sales per day. That you promote what you like and get paid at the same time is possible and without capital. There are websites like www.cj.com that are dedicated to connecting with all the affiliate companies. You make a request to the store and they accept you. There are so many industries within "affiliate marketing" that you can't even imagine. Beauty, healthy lifestyle, fitness, household products, industrial products, even digital products. You can help grow other businesses on commission while you have your regular job. You can charge from cents per click depending on the price of the product or hundreds of dollars if it is a high value product. And you say, but how am I going to create a link if nobody knows me? I barely have friends, because you have to increase the level of reach, you have to be more social. Be a person who joins groups, talks and shares because if you don't progress personally, you don't want to progress financially. You think that without lifting a finger you will be able to help more people to grow and help yourself, no. You need to scale the level of being social. There is no method that you do not do anything sitting on the couch all day and grow economically and spiritually unless you have done the right things for years that allows you that life, which is not life if you are on the couch.

If you become an Amazon affiliate and love this book, you can promote this same book for a % commission with your affiliate link. You can benefit, it's that simple, isn't the life we are living is amazin?

How many times do you not share things on your social media about products that you buy without changing anything, because it will not bother you at all to promote the same product but with an affiliate link that leaves you a percentage in commission on that same product, what is amazing?

"Drop Shipping"

Sell products without having the business or the products, you being only the mediator. It means that you set up your website with the products of the industry that make you happy, the products are from other countries and other businesses. The sales that your page generates are automated so that the sale enters the distributor and they send the product to your client. Like every business if you choose a not so hot industry or a not so hot product then things might be slow. Remember you are just investing time and energy and as time goes on you can invest money in your own product and send it to customers to dropship.

Sub Rent an Airbnb
(renting a property you don't own)

You can help people you know if they have properties they don't use. Ask if they can give you the opportunity to sub rent it to them on Airbnb or a long-term tenant. For both parties it is profit. There are people who have houses, they don't use them, they don't know the benefit they can get from their rent. There is also the person who needs someone to manage the property on these digital platforms for a % commission.

CONTENT CREATOR

Talking or creating content on something you know or like. Travel, food, products, social issues, sports, etc. The safest thing is that you have a cell phone that is worth close to a thousand dollars and that is because it has everything you need to create content 24/7. Talking about what you know and what you do can impact society in some way that they are willing to pay you for the exchange of information. Many times the same information is presented for free. People are willing to pay for information. I am one of them, I have paid for information. The fact that you impact people, people will be willing to collaborate with you with their brands or products. Look at you and me, you connected with me in some way and you're reading my book, you made an investment to connect with me by exchanging what I know. Basically the same thing I can do with you if you give me something. Raise your game, raise your knowledge and share what you know.

The most important of these online methods is to start. Find a mentor who is hard on knowledge in what you like, that helps you grow faster in the subject. Believe me that mentoring is necessary. There are people who have already been in the same place that you are now, they made many mistakes and they have the solution for you to move forward. The benefit of living in the times we are living now, people who are willing to fix problems for a cost, is the best thing that can happen in this modern age. Imagine yourself starting something in a modern time that no one has created that will take you years of knowledge, experiments to be able to achieve it. Do you think you have that patience? Do you think you have that mental stamina? To be able to execute an idea from scratch in a time that is so modern that even cars already fly and even people already fly. If you are a genius to create something that does not exist, go ahead.

In these markets that I am mentioning, they have already been there for a few years, so you do not want to be the one who does not know how it works on purpose. If you master one of these areas you can become hard on this computer but you have to want and eventually change your life. Because if you don't want to, no one will want it for you. You dream of the benefits of working from a computer anywhere in the world but you don't want to do anything to learn, that doesn't fit. Do not leave the idea in mind only and never do anything. Because if you do nothing, your future will be the same as you have today in the present. Get out of the comfort zone to fix your life, believe me these ideas are super basic for much more you can do compared to the work you have that you don't like. There are many of these online markets where you make money with more money or sometimes money with no money. But like everything there are people who break their lives because of this for not being mentally strong. They blame the market that they trying for 2 weeks. If you enter the industries in a method just to "*make money*" you will basically lose time, energy and also money and possibly your faith in your growth. It's hard for me to listen to people so much when they talk to me that *"I'm going to do this to see what happens"* . *"I'm going to try this to see what happens"*

Is that why you are going to try that thinking quickly *"let's see what happens"*? You need to go all in. You need to make it work. Climb harder, progress harder , so that your life seriously changes harder. You don't want to have your life "let's see what happens". You want to live your life to the fullest, live the best things that are for you. You have to give the maximum to the things you want to do because you cannot be lazy and have the benefits of a person who does the work and the task. When inexperienced people enter the financial markets "online" they really hit a super solid wall in the face.

MENTORING

There are people who have the solution to the mistake that you are going to make by not seeking help, don't be stubborn, don't be self-centered. There are many things that you can do on your own, but when you say "oh I don't need anyone's help, I want to do it myself I don't want to give credit to anyone" Basically that is not a strategy. There is nothing wrong with cutting the growth line, believe me, there is nothing wrong. It has too much benefit to cut the growth line.

I have invested in mentoring and I don't regret any of it because it has helped me too much even to speak, even to express myself, to be able to write this book and to be able to carry the right message. One of the most important things about this mentoring game is that you see him as a friend that you are willing to repay. A mentor friend for helping you grow. So if you think that you don't have friends to help you progress, then paying a new friend to help you progress is fantastic. I think that's magical.

DELEGATE

Another of the most important things when you are growing in entrepreneurship is to delegate tasks. If you are yourself, all the positions in your business take away the opportunity to grow completely. You have to delegate tasks because you don't know everything. You can believe that you know everything but there will always be a person who knows more than you and you will delegate to that person who knows more than you. So you can focus on another task that you master and so on, that is the strategic way for you to grow not only business-wise but also spiritually, mentally because the idea of growing in business is to grow in a healthy spiritual and mental way.

Nobody can grow in a loaded mind when you want to do everything. And believe me I've been there too. We leave our mind and our happiness for wanting to do everything at once. What is it worth to you to progress economically if it is screwing up your environment.

TURO

TURO app is the application that allows you to rent your car. The pandemic that brought the coronavirus caused travel traffic to drop. As a result many of the car rental companies went bankrupt or closed. Most had to sell their fleet of cars to survive. That gave this app a boost to position itself. Like Airbnb you can put your car up for rent for a price with your rules. You can put the minimum number of days you would like to rent it. Before the pandemic TURO was famous for having exotic cars. Now with the demand you find any car. In a saturated market right now you must know how to position yourself so as not to be in competition and have something that makes you exclusive. For that I leave you the best course to learn to be a 5-star "HOST". The website is: www.latinosenturo.com

GARAGE SALES

Another thing that is super undervalued and has a lot of potential for years. For this you need capital but not so much. Many people come out of things that they think have no value, even you have things that have value and you don't know they have it. There are many people who sell everything in their house because they have to move or renovate and they make a "garage sale" announcement on social media. There it is a prize because you are going to buy the things that you know have value. You can also do this exercise at pawn shops.

Anyway, while doing your search for used things, check how much they sell for the same thing on eBay or Amazon for the current price of new or used. This task will sometimes lead you to find $1 used items that are worth $12, that's $11 back instantly. If you practice that consistently, you can give yourself the leadership you need to keep growing. That is a method that many people say *"so I'm going to buy used things" "I don't buy used things"* Can't you buy used things to sell them? I don't understand sometimes, I don't understand people. Like garage sales, there are many people also selling used things online. It is time and energy to buy one thing to exchange it for a little more money.

THE MODERN ERA

It is not mandatory but the digital world is here to stay in such a magical era where it has made so many things easier. Everything is easier within reach, it is a benefit and at the same time a danger. If you plan well you can get a lot out of the new era, which has been a new era for a long time but maybe not for you, the digital world has to be attacked for your purpose. There is so much investment opportunity, so much invention that I would really fall short in this section of the book on all the ways money can be multiplied. Productivity is so much that thanks to the digital age you knew about this book and thanks to this book you are learning new things. If we weren't in the digital age I would have to publish this book like this: Sit in a chair at a book station and wait for someone to come up to me so I can talk about my book. Time and energy spent according to what we live now. However, now I'm doing this book by talking, I'm not even writing because I'm using voice command. I think that's why I stopped doing it two years ago so I wouldn't write it, hehe. That easy I'm going to get to your cell phone quickly, isn't that magical? The digital world can be very dangerous and vulnerable in natural disasters. A week without signal or internet is more than a natural catastrophe. The dependency is so great that you feel lost. You no longer even read the signs on the road sometimes thanks to the GPS. It has created many bums. You cannot forget to know how to be present in life, to know how to survive without the internet and with the digital way. The people of the next generation who are only going to grow with the digital age are not going to know as much as going to a place to eat and being present in life without the phone in the face. Also not many people go out to eat because with a button they can order food from the sofa at home. What it is going to bring and what is already seen in the modern digital age can bring many good things but at the same time it scares, scares if one does not prepare the mind. It doesn't matter if you are young or old, mental health is a priority and knowing how to be present in life. It is important not to let the digital age or digital businesses consume your life either, you are a life that has equal value, you are an investment that you also have to take care of.

WHY TALK ON SOCIAL MEDIA EVEN IF NO ONE KNOWS YOU?

We are living in a very social world, extra social, that I would tell you that many of the people have little privacy thanks to social networks. So that has become the "normal" when it shouldn't but there are many advantages to being social. In earlier history, if no one knew about you, they had to send you a letter in order to find out about you. Then came the radio, the telephone, the cell phone, and then the Internet. If you don't have friends or you don't have people around you, you just don't want to be social. Before, it was understandable that no one knew who you were or you simply didn't have friends, because if you were very well at home and they didn't call you or you didn't find out about the next party, you simply didn't exist. Now you have the opportunity to exist on purpose. Many people shake their hands thinking that to speak on social media you have to be famous or you have to be an "influencer" or you have something to offer specifically. The truth is no, the idea of your being in social media is to be just you, you don't have to be "someone else". You bring something to the table with your existence, with your personality, with your creativity. If you don't have creativity, be creative and start taking the first step, do it. If you need friendships or connect with people, the first thing you have to do is talk. As easy as picking up the phone and saying "Hey I'm looking for people to start a new idea" or "I'm looking for people to raise my mental level" those who want to share will contact you. Maybe at first, if you are not a social person, then you will not receive a quick message about what you want, but once you do it and do it and do it, believe me, someone will answer you. The first few times I started talking on social media it was basically easy because I knew I wasn't talking to anyone.

I still use that method, I speak as if I am not speaking to anyone specific but at the same time as if I am speaking to someone close to me to keep it genuine. In order for me to carry the message, my mission has always been that if I speak, I can reach a person who needs me due to the fact that most have the phone 70% of their time. Not everyone has the best people around and that I provide a message of support or how I feel. Doing it can inspire or accelerate the creativity of a person to feel better or even worse maybe because there is everything in the world. But the idea is to raise your voice. I remember myself being alone without communication with anyone looking for solutions on my own, trying to have a better quality of life, waiting for things to come to me, until I realized that things do not work that way. We have to start finding them. Basically, if I hadn't reached the necessary people along the way, I would still be stuck without knowing anybody in my way. You never know what can happen if you never take action based on the future you want to have. However, speaking up, connecting with people, having friendships, etc. I have met people with big hearts, I have known a brutally new culture, friendships with another type of thought, enjoying the different ideas between us and respecting each other. All of this has helped me increase my empathic capacity because when you tell your story there is always someone who also has a story to tell you. It is a super beautiful world to be able to connect with people who are just as wise and interesting as you or not so wise. But your being able to connect with people as such is a blessing. Start simple, start talking about how you feel, greeting good morning, good afternoon, what did you do today, if you liked or did not like the day, let people know who you are. Do not present yourself as you are not either, be you and as you have consistency in communicating who you are, people will find consistency in speaking to you. Do you think I would have known before that today I was going to receive messages from people around the world of support? Also hate messages to be honest. However, that is the impact of raising my voice because if I would not do it, those people who speak to me would not know that I exist. Those are the fruits, however I have to be clear, my mission has never been for people to find out that I exist on purpose. When I was first doing it and until now, I only try to communicate with people who feel lonely, people who maybe feel abandoned. Because many times I felt that way and that is why it is my call to do so. I do not seek fame nor do I want fame in general. I can live in peace with who I am today and do my will whenever I can reach someone or not. The same thing you can look for when talking on social media, you can simply be you, not looking for fame, not looking for recognition, simply leaving your mark on how to help a person. You can help so much with a solution to a problem and it doesn't have to be perfect for you to help someone. How many times has YouTube not gotten you out of trouble on how to do something thanks to people who dared to take a video of the solution. Look at this example, You can have a day in which you had a lot of things to do and everything went wrong. However, on the way home, you saw a person who had a tire burst and you decided to help him and everything went well. It is the best example that I can tell you that life does not have to be perfect for you to be able to help someone. You just have to have a good heart, learn to have a good heart and be empathic. Empathy is something that is not discussed much and I love it. Once you understand empathy, we understand how people can or cannot help each other. Search social media for people who have your best personal interest in improving because if you use your social media only for entertainment, to watch videos of problems, videos of laughter or videos of negative news, then you are simply entertaining your eyes and not advancing in anything . That is very similar to people who spend all day watching TV, that for me is slowly killing the mind. If you want to grow as a person, then you have to take care of what you watch and listen to and who you follow. See that they are looking for the same thing that you want, to grow as a person, that they are speaking as you want to speak, that they are doing and exercising what you want. Not with the interest of copying it, it is simply to sow the seed in you and you can create your own path. Why something that is getting confused in this new generation in social media is wanting to see people as competition or see people as comparison. There should really be no comparison neither in social media nor in the present world where you have a presence around you. You don't have to compare yourself in social media with those who have better things or worse things, who have a better quality of life or not, because basically it is an ancient culture thinking of comparing yourself. The one who compares himself in social media does not love himself. Use social media to heal yourself, not to get sick. Basically, those who do not have control of what they are looking for on social media end up infected in the comparison, psychologically affected thinking that they do not have a good life that they can share and that is wrong. I think that the more organic you are and be yourself, the more impact you have on people's lives so that you can gain their trust when it comes to connecting. Being yourself doesn't put you under the pressure that you have to pretend to someone you're not. It makes me sad that many people have to pretend only to have a life in social media and not enjoy real life outside of social media. I am one of those who prefer to have my real life, whether raw or not, if I comb my hair or not, if I have the best clothes or not. That keeps my mind healthy since

I don't have to live for someone's specific tastes.

Social media has helped me a lot to find mentors, friends who have been able to help me be the person I am. Pursue the career I have, communicate in the way I communicate, express my feelings and look for destinations to travel. Social media gets a lot out of it in terms of growth. I don't use social media as a term to get infected. Anything that infects my eyes and ears, I block it. I unfollow it. I don't allow something on social media to take me out of focus or entertain me. My focus is growth when I am free. Being in social media allows me to see people I haven't seen for a long time, what they are doing with their lives, if they are having a good or bad time, if they need me. It is a blessing in the way that one can be close today even though people are far away. If you are not benefiting right now from your social media you should start right now, take out the phone and say that you are reading my book, that you feel good or bad about my book and if you recommend it or not. Start with that video. You started with something. It doesn't matter if it's good or bad, it doesn't matter if it's perfect, it doesn't matter if you have light or not, if your phone is of quality or not. The important thing is the step you are going to take can change the course of your life completely. Then you have to have the goal of continuing to grow to impact your discipline every day. A piece of communication is an invitation to who you want to be and the person you are going to become.

MENTAL AND EMOTIONAL HEALTH.

You have heard about emotional feelings, empathy, but I know that many people do not understand this topic as well as other topics that I am gonna talk about. Even if they know or have heard it before, they don't fully understand it. This is the issue where it's super vulnerable for a lot of people. In order to find emotional peace they have to find themselves. You have to know what your identity is, what you carry, what you like and what you don't like as a person for you. Not as a person for other people.

Like yourself as a person as if no one else existed in the world for a moment. Just for a moment, we don't have to be so selfish either, we don't want to feed the ego. Once you identify your identity, you can identify what is bad for you and what is good for you.

Exercise time!

You are going to take a notebook. You are going to start writing what you like on one side and what you don't like on the other side. Elsewhere, what would you like to do with your life. You are going to evaluate those things that you like with that you do not like. Ask yourself if they are leading you to what you would like to do differently in your life. Remember to write everything as a first person. We are talking in emotional and personal terms about what makes you happy and what does not make you happy. That is the first exercise to take your life seriously because many people want to take their life seriously but they are not able to write a notebook that makes them happy or not. I don't understand how they want to take life seriously. Because you can have most of the things that make you happy around you and still not be happy inside of you. However, you have not reached where you want to go but you are happy and you do not know it. All this comes as a result of not making a personal evaluation of identity and emotional peace.

With all the distractions plus social media and many things that I explained to you a moment ago, it can be what harms you as a person and knowing it. When I was talking to you about comparing yourself with other people, it is something that can harm your peace. If you are a self-centered person who does not have empathy for others, it can also harm you.

What if you found some way to be able to feel good for others and not bad with others or bad with your life because others are doing well and you are not? Honestly, *who really sets the rules for who is doing well and who is not doing well based on emotional terms?* Have you thought about that? What is behind every social media and behind every heart?

Who are you to identify other people if they are doing well or not? Yes, you don't know the answer. I know, it's basically, why are you paying attention to other people's emotions and not paying attention to your own emotions? Which are the ones that matter!

What you are carrying 24 hours inside your head you cannot escape. Why don't you use your head to give her love and attention first? Avoid the comparison of paying attention to others for a moment in order to achieve that emotional peace that you are looking for, whatever life you have. Once you do the notebook exercise, the next thing is to take action on the things you are going to do in order to get to the place you want to be or the person you want to be. This is the most difficult exercise when it comes to progress, because many people want to progress and feel good about progress from the beginning. They don't want to suffer, they don't want to shed a tear or anything and progress is basically emotional ups and downs. Your power to cope with what is happening to you is to have control of yourself. Neither progress or life are rose flowers so that you want to undertake a new idea, embark on a new path and that it goes perfect. Super easy and smiling every day from the first day. That would just be a fantasy. But, if you work on your emotional peace and you put control of your progress is more bearable. Accepting the ups and downs, your emotional peace is more bearable and that is the first step to true growth.

Your emotional peace begins with you. What you don't like around you should be removed. The people who do not make up anything in your life you have to remove them. They are difficult steps to take, I know. Many people get too attached to people or get too attached to things. They don't let go of people or things either. Taking action on that difficult decision is what will take you on the road to peace of mind. Get out of those things you don't need that are leading you to failure. Get out of the people who are leading you to failure. Getting out of love is going to take you where you want to be and one of them is to be happy with yourself. It can be even painful to cut emotional attachment but it is WORTH IT. You may feel a lot of ups and downs at first but ups and downs and how everything is not going to change overnight. With this, what you are going to do is push yourself up completely and your emotional peace. It is a great step that you cut with those things that are holding you back.

One of the most complicated things is when you practice being a good human being. When you are a good human being, you want everyone around you to be good. You want to grow up with people you are attached to, but do these people around you want the same with you? That's what you should ask yourself because if you want to grow up with people who don't want to grow up with you. Basically you're wasting your time. If you want to progress and the people around you don't want to progress, they end up being an anchor for you. And if they are an anchor for you, they end up affecting your emotional peace because you cannot achieve what you want to achieve basically because you do not want to let go of the chain of attachment.

I have had to let go of people from my life completely. Creating a super distance and a barrier at the same time for wanting to find more of my peace. I had anchors without knowing that I had anchors for having a good heart. I do not want to see it and I do not want to understand it. It becomes normal and it shouldn't become normal that you want to progress and people around you want to be an anchor instead of a seed. If they are not seed, your emotional peace is affected and you can stop being the great person you are because you sink emotionally and you don't know how long you can be on that dark side emotionally. Without being able to achieve your goals that you are looking for so much because you do not want to take off. It is too costly not to have emotional peace. Life constantly stops you completely.

My experience separating myself from people for my emotional health was one of the most vulnerable in my life. Because of the fact that I care about people. I care about people and I want people to do well in life. So staying away from people for my mental health is not an easy decision. It makes it more difficult when they are loved ones that you are used to seeing and feeling. I made the first decision to get as far away as possible from people who were affecting my emotional health by not contributing anything to my progress. It was difficult at first but the recovery was so fast and the benefits have been so many that it has been one of the best decisions in my life. There is no way back. It does not mean that I wish these people ill or hold a grudge against them.

Wishing evil and holding a grudge is nothing for peace of mind, it's not me. I only respect the distance because it is healthy for me. Having people who affect my peace my north is affected and I can't, that is very expensive. Not taking care of your mental health is expensive because it harms productivity. Usually these people that you want to distance yourself from, are the ones who always want to attack you or who want to see you emotionally badly. From the front they see you well and from the back they even talk about how you are going to fail or even die. They see your progress and they envy you, they just can't stand that you are always set for progress and sanity. It gets too confusing trying to explain to a person your mission or your way of seeing life and demanding that they support you.

Is it better for you to move away. The time that is wasted explaining what you want, what you think, what you believe in life and that they understand or accept or value you. It is time and energy that is not recovered. Time cannot be recovered, it is something that must be valued every day. As a priority, I tend to value my life every day and even more so when life matters so much to you. When you walk away from these toxic people, they will do everything possible to make you look like "the bad guy" because you left or abandoned them. They will say that you are a person who does not care about humanity and all that kind of stuff. I don't see anything wrong with people having to abandon people to meet goals if they don't contribute and top of all, destructive..

Fight for your dreams no matter what you have to sacrifice.

These people you should stay away from are the ones you do a thousand things for them and they don't remember and judge you for just one. They don't value the things you do for them because they lack recognition and empathy. When you leave that toxic environment and accept that you are not going to turn back, it is healthier. It is much healthier than any disease cure. Not taking care of your mental health because of being tied to toxic people becomes an emotional illness. Like a vicious circle. Difficult to cure because it is in your head and you carry your head 24 hours. This disease has a cure. You have to take your things and go, you will not regret it. The people you have to get away from are these people who do not bring anything to the table. You will realize when you walk away, because you will not miss anything. Because there is nothing to miss. The only thing you're going to miss based on my experience is how good you were to those people. Not only because someone doesn't bring something to the table, you're going to cut it. It's that they also take what you bring to the table, they don't value it. If you are trying to build your inner peace and they take away too much of your peace, they are basically subtracting from your equation. Your mission is to multiply and strengthen yourself, do not allow them to subtract from you. It takes a lot of work to progress emotionally and in your personal goals. I say again, I don't regret having said *BYE* after years of loaded environments and bad atmosphere that I almost lost faith in myself. Those are the times that I came to hear that I was not going to achieve anything. That I was going to end up alone. That was like wishing me dead with those comments. The most difficult moments of my life were not my fault. It was the fault of irresponsible people who due to lack of empathy, lack of knowledge did not know how to provide what a quality human being can provide. It was my fault if I didn't make the decision to walk away. But I don't want to carry the blame, I didn't want to carry it any more and right now I don't. I am not alone either and I have achieved more than I could imagine from where I come from and the list does not end. More than anything achieving happiness and peace of mind goes above and beyond anything you can achieve. That is something no one can take away from me. The rest can be recovered but if peace is lost it is difficult to restore. Now I have my peace at the highest level thanks to walking away and putting myself in the right place where people value me and add me. If you want to have emotional peace, in addition to evaluating the people around you,

What is the most draining thing when looking for your emotional peace?

Besides the wrong people, *what are you doing with your life and your body?*

What are your eyes consuming?

What are your ears consuming?

What are your decisions each day?

Write these questions in your notebook and answer them. Because if you're not constantly watching and listening for better emotional health, then basically you don't want to be. You're not going to make it, that's cheating.

As a result of the situations that I have had in my life that affected me emotionally for a while, I found a peaceful moment. It was running 2 to 5 miles a day. It doesn't matter if it was Sunday or if it was 11 PM. I was just running to find my shelter inside. And I say I ran because now I only run 2 miles. In a chapter of my story I start to have problems with my heart. Those problems stopped me from running, which was my medicine. That's where my real emotional challenge began without planning. After I had heart problems I could no longer be the same running and

I entered into new challenges of getting to know myself again from the inside. And when I say meet myself again I speak in emotional terms because I have always known my other external goals outside my body and I have always executed them. But emotional peace is another kind of important goal, a little more vulnerable. After the heart event it took me six years to understand how my identity was stolen by not finding running as a shelter. Before the heart event, I had been running for 10 years. I began to look for my shelter in other things. I looked in other areas and in many places where I couldn't find it until finally finding it and being able to explain it today. Not being able to run like before, I began to be a person afraid of dying from the heart. Being afraid of dying from the heart I was afraid to run and feel my heartbeat increasing. However I was present in my life, living on my own terms and fulfilling my dreams all good, but emotionally I was entering a dark side. For not having the shelter I was looking for, which was running.

I looked for alternatives to be able to be active and to be able to raise my heart rate to lead a healthy life and all of them were unsuccessful. Because the first time I felt my heart beating I had to stop. This over time was affecting my physical health. It was a new challenge to understand why it was being affected. It wasn't that I wasn't training, it wasn't that I wasn't eating healthy, it was that I was having a bad habit of something. Something that didn't allow me to be the person I was before I had heart problems. Six years later I can say that what I had built was fear and from fear I built obesity and from fear I built insecurity and from fear I looked for the answer to being physically and emotionally healthy again. I couldn't believe that I was achieving so many things in my life, living to the fullest and my physical health was deteriorating because of my fear affecting my emotional peace. I started with exercises of acceptance and gratitude. I start the day saying thanks for being alive and giving me the opportunity to meet me again. I looked for help from professionals, who at first gave me alternatives that I was already using but those alternatives were not working for my physics. My fitness goal was to get back to my healthy weight. I had already improved from being out of hypertension and I returned to suffer hypertension due to obesity. Yes, I have had high blood pressure since I was 20 years old due to the abuse of alcohol. With a lot of effort, quitting alcohol and exercising had already improved. Then my hypertension returned due to obesity because I can go months without drinking. I knew it wasn't the alcohol. A dark moment in my life but not without hope, not without that I had to find the solution to that problem that was happening in my body. Many times I thought it was the thyroid, I did labs and nothing. Many times I thought it was diabetes but the labs were fine anyway. I was just afraid. A fear that I built and really everything that I was living, my desire to live was to the fullest, just like now.

I decided to do some heart studies one more time. I explained my fear of the heart that I had not talked about. I don't know if it was true or not but he basically told me something that really shot the fear away. He told me: *"Your heart is fine, try to do everything possible to get your life back on track. Nothing will happen to you for exercising. Try to do exercises as you used to do obviously moderately. Do not be afraid that something is going to happen to you because with this study that we have just carried out, your heart is not vulnerable."* Apparently after so much time of taking care of my heart without raising the heart rate, it got stronger. Believe me the last thing I wanted was to harm him with obesity. That same day the chain of fear was broken. Once breaking the chain of fear, I became emotionally stable again to believe in myself. Six years in fear and in a year I returned to my ideal weight. I have not been able to feel better. Achieving this peace emotionally is a happiness that cannot be bought.

At the level that I gained weight, I had never reached so much weight in my life, I saw it impossible to be me again. But I never gave up. I never gave up looking for the answer. Not only physically, but also for my emotional peace. I knew it was hurting me. I couldn't be more obese in the future. I have always loved exercise, it has been my shelter to be emotionally stable for many years. For more than 15 years. This had to happen to me to get to know myself again and create the strongest emotional quality of life, of what I already knew. I was just doing exercises halfway out of fear, fear of feeling my heart beat. I had PTSD from the pain I suffered when I had heart problems. That's why I tell you the exercise of taking care of your peace should never stop because if I hadn't done my daily exercise, I would have become obese and I wouldn't even think about it. Accept that I am obese and ignore the situation, it's not me. When you work on your emotional peace why does it matter to you, you are aware and you know what affects you. If it was affecting me that I was gaining weight in an inexplicable way, then basically I had to look for a solution and I found it.

WHAT YOU HAVE INSIDE YOUR DIGESTIVE SYSTEM

In this matter it is always good to seek professional help to determine what may be happening specifically with your body. In my case, professional help did not help me make the decisions I made to improve my physical health and my obesity. They just helped me lose my fear. After being so long gaining weight and gaining weight. To a level where I couldn't take it anymore. I needed to find a new alternative. Within those alternatives I became vegan for a while. I stopped eating meat every day along with my exercise and continued to gain weight. I thought that I had diabetes but the doctors told me that I did not have diabetes and that everything is fine. But it wasn't right, the mirror told me that something wasn't right inside of me. I needed to change and had changed my diet to the same as before the heart problem. That diet had been super effective for my body type before. With a new weight, a new mentality, I accepted that my body was contaminated. From something other than the fear I had of my heart rate. So I searched so that I could give my body a restoration of the toxins that it had. I became more and more serious that this had to change soon. For a moment I leaned towards that I had to have bariatric surgery or that I had to have surgery in some way. Once I realized that my obesity was getting out of proportion I didn't see it stopping in the near future. And after doing so much searching I realized that the contamination was in the supermarket purchases. They were supposed to be healthy and it turns out that most of the labels that carry a "Healthy Branding" carry too much hidden sugar and gluten. You think you are eating a low caloric intake but those few calories are very high in sugar and sugar is converted to insulin and insulin is converted to fat. So every time I walk into the supermarket and see all the shelves I see mountains of sugar behind every product. The first step I took to change my diet and be able to give my body a restoration was to go straight to real food. Real food is everything that is not frozen and packaged. Everything possible that I didn't have a preservative or something that would keep further infecting my body. I reduce the meat portion due to the fact that it contaminates my body less if I reduce it. Meats have a high percentage of fat plus contamination from the farm. But it was not enough to give my body a reset. I changed my meat protein for fresh fish.

However, I did not see anything changing yet significantly. I continued my investigation of knowing my obese body to be out of contamination. I decided to do things to get more serious about this restoration of my physical health. I start to learn more about fasting for benefit or risk. I limited myself to fasting before because for me it was always that the longer you go without eating, the slower your metabolism becomes. I was wrong. Fasting your body with just water gives your body a chance to restore cells and flush out toxins naturally. Nothing to do with slowing down the metabolism. Yes, you will damage the metabolism if you spend unstable hours without eating without a plan. I started fasting in an organized way at the same time most of the time in order to maintain a balance in my body. The benefits of fasting are better than even modern medicine in some cases. When you eat, your body processes the food. But when you are fasting your body looks for energy from body fat if there is no food. It speeds up your metabolism better by the way your intestines are cleaned. I started with 12 hours, then 15 and I am currently on an 18 hour fast every day. This has allowed me to reach autophagy. Autophagy is a natural regeneration mechanism that occurs in our body at the cellular level. It reduces the probability of contracting certain diseases and prolongs life expectancy. Once balancing my body with fasting I was losing my first 20 pounds in several months. Best of all, I was enjoying the process, I began to feel more energized and my vision clearer every day. But I kind of hit a stone in the road in weight loss again. Thanks to some friends I have, who are angels, they guided me about the benefits of the enema. It was very likely that although I had changed my diet, my body was not completely clean. I knew about the enema of coffee because I knew that people with constipation needed an enema. Also enema has many benefits better than medicine. Can prevent alcoholism, allergies, arthritis, asthma, back pain, bad breath, bloating, dirty tongue, colitis, constipation, nicotine damage, fatigue, gas, headaches, high cholesterol, high blood pressure, indigestion, insomnia, joint problems, liver failure, cancer, loss of concentration, mental disorders, infections, nasal congestion, skin problems, and ulcerative colitis. I took action and it was not an easy process. A not easy process because something new. Today I am grateful that I was able to give my body the benefit of a coffee enema and be able to continue losing more pounds making a total of 70 pounds to be able to reach my ideal weight. The weight that I always liked being my healthy weight. I wrote it and I don't believe it went from 240lbs to 170lbs. Although you should not compete against weight because weight is just a number. It is how you look and more how you feel. The great combination between cleansing my body and giving it real food. I started to burn more calories than I was taking in, which further helped me reach my goal. I use the "Fastic" app to learn from fasting the paid version that helped me learn more. The "MyFitnessPal" app to know how many calories you were consuming based on what you ate. I decided to eat 700 calories in my eating window by coming off the fast and burning 1500 calories in exercise. So I was able to be in a caloric deficit in order to lower my body fat and eventually my weight. I confess that I made my cheat meals Pizza, Hamburgers and other stuff and they didn't affect my goal. It came to my mind that obesity was my destiny because I was over 30 years old. Another myth debunked. The longest I've lasted without eating junk food was 35 days. 35 days is a long time but when you enjoy what you're eating you don't realize it. You have to enjoy life. Eating real food isn't boring, it's even fresher and tastier than a restaurant. If you know how to make yourself the things you like with real unprocessed food. Of course, I spend more time when it comes to making food because everything has to be prepared and everything has to be measured in order to have the amount that my body needs to be able to stay in the area that I want. The time has been worth it and the sacrifice too. When you eat the same thing most days it makes you anxious to eat something different. The anxiety of eating something different is relative, it is simply that you do not want to cook. That's the secret I wish I had known ever since I started gaining weight. But everything comes at the right time and at the right moment. The universe is beautiful and I learned too much self-love when I was obese.

Meeting my goals every day even knowing that I was working on my emotional and physical peace at the same time was a challenge. Now that I know the secret of how my body works and with real food I won't give up the fast or the weekly enema because the intestine develops bacteria and toxins as it pleases. Therefore, no matter how healthy you eat, you have to constantly cleanse yourself in order to keep your body 100% healthy. Once you are super healthy, your body is clean. Mentally clean also because you achieved that goal that was destroying your peace of mind or trying to fight with it. That is how I feel. I feel more energetic since I wake up, I sleep much better. For the first time in a long time I feel whole better than I was. As I said before, I thought I was not going to come back. I thought I was not going to be able to lose weight the way I wanted because for me I was doing everything. I did extreme diets like eating only salad along with drinking a gallon and a half of water a day and nothing in my body changed. Even when I was "vegan" eating vegan products. Vegan products are high in sodium which didn't really work for me. The enemies of food are gluten, fat, sugar and sodium. If you move away from these four things in food, the more you exercise, the closer you will get to the goal. Eating real food helps you avoid having to read supermarket labels. But YES you have to read every label of what you buy. I know that it takes time to buy food because you have to go to the supermarket every week to keep it fresh. And you have to prepare them from scratch. The change is tedious if you eat many processed things that come in packages to change for things that you have to prepare yourself. But it is more tedious to live in obesity believe me.

Living in sorrow and living in an unhealthy way is the worst. The feeling of your body does not respond because you are not healthy it can make you impatient. If you get sick often, it is that in your body there is something to heal. Since I made this change I haven't had a cold or sinus that gave me a hard time in bed for two weeks. That no longer exists. There are people who accept themselves as obese and continue to eat the same bacteria that they eat all the time. They don't think about the damage they do to their health and to those around them if they don't lose weight. They are at risk of falling into the hospital or worse, death. So if you want to awaken the genius in you, start by taking care of your emotional health and also your physical health, you will have a better performance. Even feel better because that way you feel better your decisions are even better. Lack of weight control will lead to depression. Depression is going to lead you to have days that are lower than high due to the fact that depression works that way. Depression is unstable. In order for you to improve your physical, emotional health you combat depression at the same time. You have to have a lot of discipline to do things because they suit you and not because you feel like it. If you are in depression most of the time you don't feel like doing anything. You will not want to cook, exercise, much less watch what you consume. In order for your power to achieve it is by taking action. Whether you're sad or not getting out of bed to cook. Whether or not you feel like going to the gym or training at home. Find a sport that you have always liked and practice it. In this process of body changing I started playing tennis without knowing. I fell in love with tennis because it is a sport that seems easy but it is not. It is a sport that requires your whole body to be in sync in order to enjoy it. It's more you against you than you against your opponent. It was what I needed. There are different times for each person, there are those who help genetics and there are those who don't. For people who are not helped by genetics like me, we have to work twice as hard because genetics is well present in the physiology of how your body is going to be.

THE MISSION

Just be happy, let others be happy in what they believe. If you are a person who likes to feel power over things and people, let go of the ego. The ego makes you feel like you deserve everything. With ego you will believe that the solutions will come to your door. You put in mind "that one day your success will come" when it is success that is waiting for you. Don't force things, if they don't happen when you want, don't stop fighting. If you have a bad day and you have a lot of courage, take a piece of paper and write all the blessings you have in your day. You don't see blessings with courage, but start giving thanks because you are alive, you have a bed to sleep in. You have a table to eat. You have the opportunity to say "I love you" because you have a voice. You get to hear that they love you because you are blessed to hear. You can hug someone because you have full arms. You can get places because you have legs. And if I continue, I won't finish. Today even if you are disabled but have life, you have a reason to keep fighting. Life is simple, don't complicate it. Allow them to love you and help you when you need it. Look for the best version of you every day. Live the present, forget the past. There is a promising future waiting for you. Be you, love yourself before loving other people. Your life will change by the steps you take each day.

I WANT TO TALK TO YOU

Find the Facebook Group "Awaken the Genius in you". I want to meet every person who reads this book to the end. I want you to be able to share your story too and be respected.

Follow me on Instagram: @reyanthony_

You can follow some of my projects on Instagram
@Wolftradespr
@Genuveskin

In memory of:
Mirca L. Santana Rodriguez
Fly high my queen, Rest in Peace

REY ANTHONY

www.ingramcontent.com/pod-product-compliance
Lightning Source LLC
Chambersburg PA
CBHW071502220526
45472CB00003B/884